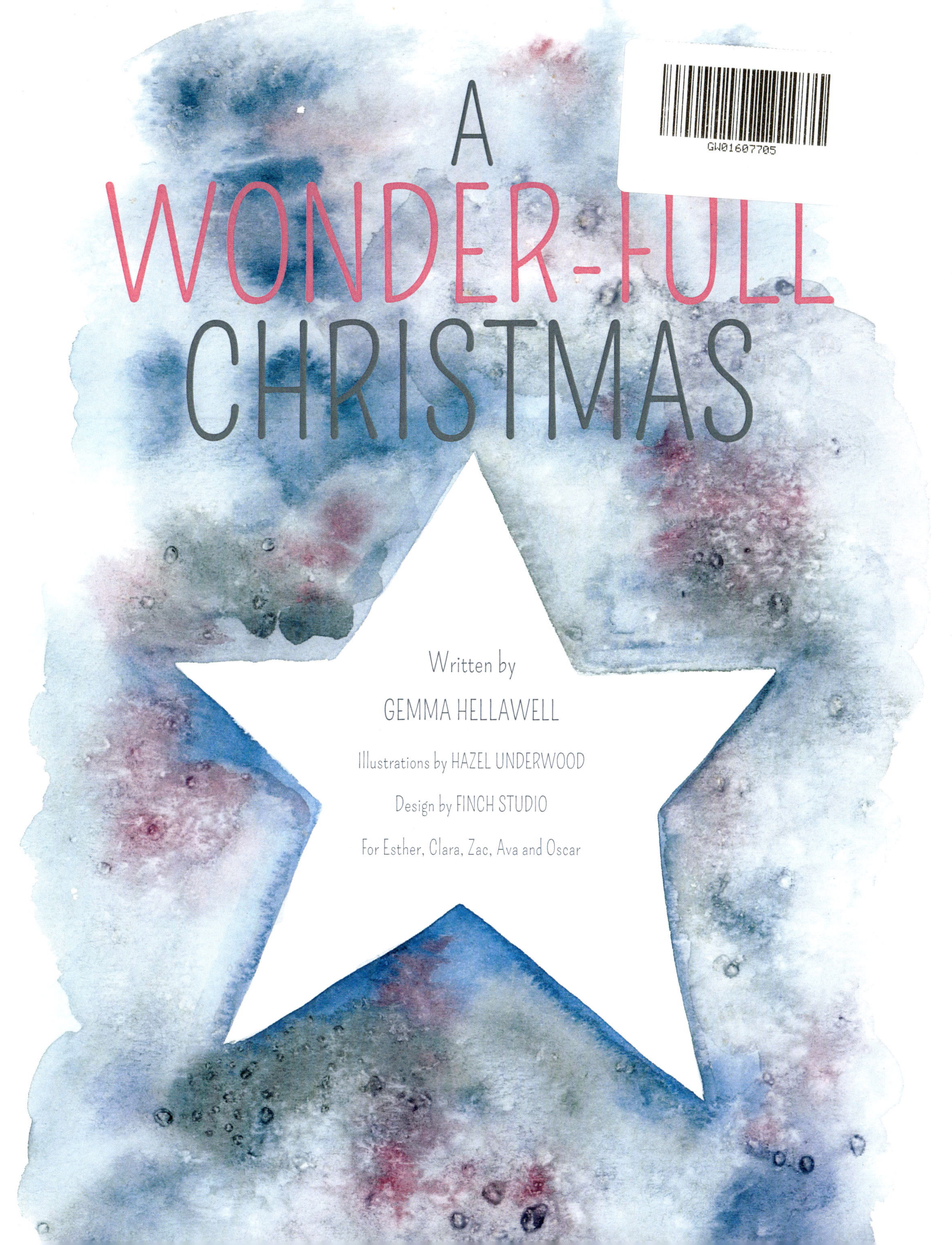

A WONDER-FULL CHRISTMAS

Written by

GEMMA HELLAWELL

Illustrations by HAZEL UNDERWOOD

Design by FINCH STUDIO

For Esther, Clara, Zac, Ava and Oscar

It's a tale that's been told countless times -
A baby born in a manger with all the animals around,
But when have you ever really stopped to think
How incredible that story really is?

A baby king born in a nowhere town
Celebrated with a new star and not a crown,

With shepherds, not royalty, as honoured guests
And a bed fit for animals instead of the best.

But we're racing ahead, we
need to slow down
Because our tale begins a
long way from this town.
This story was written by
God and not man
And this day was the unveiling
of His master plan
To make a way for God and
man to be friends,
For us to know of
his love and to have life
without end.

And so strange to us as each
detail now seems
It was all part of a plan beyond
our wildest dreams.

This babe-king who'd
been there at the start of
creation
Had come as a servant
to save every nation.

The stage had been set long before Jesus came
God had whispered the plan to each generation by name.
Those who had heard were waiting expectantly
For a Prince of Peace to come and set them free.

It took many years but God's
timing is perfect
And when everything was just
right, God said "go" to his project.
He started by searching for a
heart that was pure
Someone who knew of the plans
he had in store.

He found a girl, just a teen, with
a true loving heart
And sent an angel with a special
message to impart.
Gabriel was a sight filling Mary
with fear,
But his message was of love and
of God coming near.
"You have been chosen," he said
to the girl,
"To carry the King, the one that
will save the world."
So Jesus was conceived by
miracle not man,
By God doing what only he can.

Just think how you'd feel if
you were that girl
Trying hard to explain to
Joseph the deal.

At first he was keen to just
walk away
Until he saw the same angel
who convinced him to stay.
This brave man agreed and
signed up to the plan
Playing his part in God's story
to rescue man.

And so the baby grew and the parents got ready
As much as they could for the arrival from heaven.
Then a curve ball was thrown, they had a census to sign
The timing couldn't be worse but they mustn't decline.
So the expectant parents packed themselves on their way
And headed to Bethlehem looking for somewhere to stay.

And again, for just a moment, imagine it was you -
About to give birth without even a clue
Of where you might sleep or where the baby would be born
Mary's heart must have been overflowing with concern.

But our God provides and an outhouse was found
A stable where cattle, horses and sheep abound.

It was there, amongst nature, in the last place you'd look
That the King of Creation his first breath took.
Just as they'd been told they named the babe Jesus
Because he had come to the earth to save us.

For this special baby
it was no surprise
That many visitors began
to arrive.

But the names that appeared on
God's VIP guest list
Were unusual, in fact they were
most unexpected.

First shepherds, the ones others didn't want around.
On the hills outside Bethlehem was where they could be found.

Hunkered down for another cold night
When all of a sudden the sky was alight
With the most astounding sight they had ever seen -
It was hard to believe that it wasn't a dream.
Angels sang and they danced as they loudly implored,
"He is here! The King's been born. Go and see and adore."

And they did and they found him
just as they'd been told.
Seeing God as a baby was a
sight to behold.

These men were changed by
this first encounter
And left telling the world all
they'd seen ever after.

But it wasn't just shepherds
God invited to visit
The God of the universe made this
a cosmic event.

A new star shone bright in a sky that
was studied
By wise men in the East who then
felt encouraged
To follow this star so they too could adore,
They left on their journey not knowing what
was in store.

It took months, if not years to reach their destination
And when they got close there was much deliberation,
They began to believe that they must have misread
Because it was to the back-water Bethlehem that their star led.

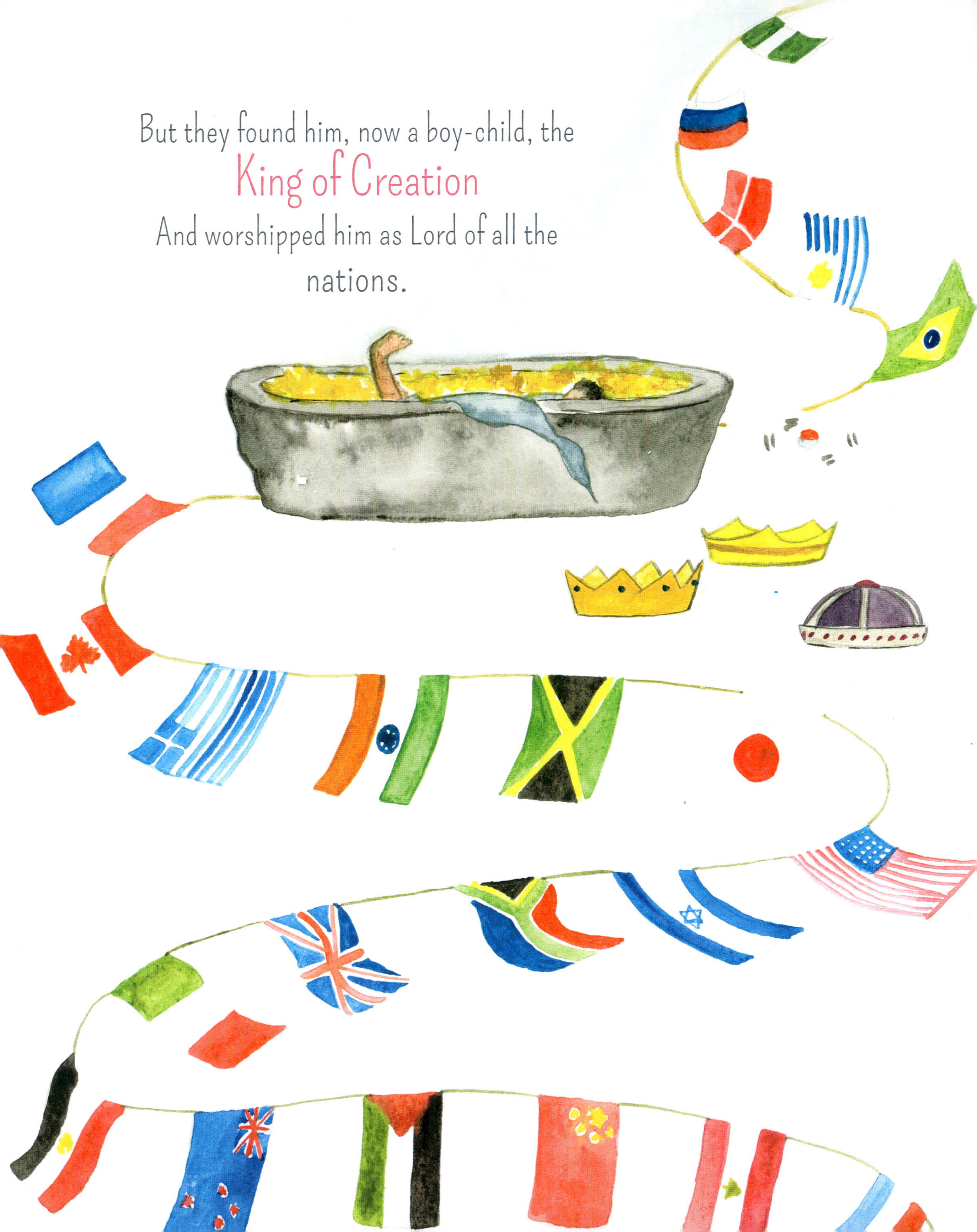

But they found him, now a boy-child, the
King of Creation
And worshipped him as Lord of all the
nations.

They brought him three gifts
we could easily ignore,
But each had a message, a sign
of what was in store;
Gold because this little boy
was a king,
Then Frankincense to show
that his death would bring
Us back into friendship with our
perfect creator
Jesus stands in the gap
acting as our mediator.

And finally myrrh which is used for embalming
A sign of the sacrifice that was coming -

Because you see it wasn't just his birth that
would have such significance,
The whole of Jesus' life was designed to
make a difference.

The child grew into a man who set people free
Healing bodies, bringing hope, so that everyone could see
That God really did want to know us all personally
And to give us new life to enjoy eternally.

So this isn't just a nice story to tell at this time of year,
It has eternal significance if you will really hear.

Let God speak to your heart of the
love that he has

And really open your heart to
Jesus this Christmas.

'For to us a child is born, to us a son is given... he will be called Wonderful Counsellor, Mighty God, Everlasting Father, Prince of Peace.' Isaiah 9:6